50 Family-Friendly Dinners Everyone Will Love

By: Kelly Johnson

Table of Contents

- Spaghetti Bolognese
- Chicken Alfredo
- Beef Tacos
- BBQ Chicken Sliders
- Meatloaf with Mashed Potatoes
- Chicken Parmesan
- Homemade Pizza
- Sloppy Joes
- Shepherd's Pie
- Beef and Bean Chili
- Chicken Stir-Fry
- Beef and Cheese Enchiladas
- Grilled Cheese and Tomato Soup
- Fish Sticks with Fries
- Spaghetti Carbonara
- Chicken Fajitas
- Macaroni and Cheese
- Teriyaki Chicken with Rice
- Chicken Nuggets and Veggies
- Stuffed Bell Peppers
- Sausage and Peppers
- Lasagna
- Turkey Meatballs with Marinara
- Pulled Pork Sandwiches
- Veggie Fried Rice
- Beef Tacos with Guacamole
- Roast Chicken with Potatoes
- Baked Ziti
- Shrimp Scampi
- Grilled Chicken Caesar Salad
- Breakfast for Dinner (Pancakes, Eggs, Bacon)
- Beef Burritos
- BBQ Ribs with Corn on the Cob
- Chicken and Rice Casserole
- Sliders with Sweet Potato Fries

- Beef Stroganoff
- Chicken Quesadillas
- Veggie Pizza
- Turkey Burgers
- Chicken Tenders with Honey Mustard
- Beef and Vegetable Kabobs
- Eggplant Parmesan
- Chicken and Broccoli Alfredo Bake
- Meatball Subs
- Beef and Spinach Lasagna Roll-Ups
- Chicken Pot Pie
- Taco Salad
- Pork Schnitzel with Mashed Potatoes
- Chicken Enchilada Casserole
- Sweet and Sour Chicken with Rice

Classic Spaghetti Bolognese

Ingredients:

- 2 tbsp olive oil
- 1 onion, finely chopped
- 2 cloves garlic, minced
- 1 carrot, grated or finely chopped
- 2 celery stalks, finely chopped
- 1 lb (450g) ground beef (or a mix of beef and pork)
- 1 can (14 oz) crushed tomatoes
- 2 tbsp tomato paste
- 1/2 cup red wine (optional)
- 1 cup beef broth
- 1 tsp dried oregano
- 1 tsp dried basil
- 1/2 tsp salt
- 1/4 tsp black pepper
- 1/4 tsp sugar (optional)
- 1/4 cup whole milk or cream (optional, for creaminess)
- 1 lb (450g) spaghetti
- Freshly grated Parmesan cheese, for serving (optional)

Instructions:

1. **Cook the vegetables**: Heat olive oil in a large pan over medium heat. Add the chopped onion and garlic, cooking until soft and fragrant, about 3-4 minutes. Add the grated carrot and chopped celery, and cook for another 3 minutes until the vegetables are tender.
2. **Brown the meat**: Add the ground beef (and pork, if using) to the pan. Break it up with a wooden spoon, and cook until browned, about 6-8 minutes. Drain excess fat if necessary.
3. **Add the liquids and seasonings**: Stir in the tomato paste, crushed tomatoes, and red wine (if using). Add the beef broth, oregano, basil, salt, pepper, and sugar. Stir to combine and bring to a simmer.
4. **Simmer**: Lower the heat and let the sauce simmer for at least 30 minutes, stirring occasionally. If you have more time, simmer for up to 1-2 hours for a richer flavor. Stir in the milk or cream if you want a creamier sauce.
5. **Cook the spaghetti**: While the sauce is simmering, cook the spaghetti according to the package directions. Drain the pasta, reserving a cup of pasta water.

6. **Combine and serve**: Toss the cooked spaghetti with the Bolognese sauce, adding reserved pasta water if needed to loosen the sauce. Serve with grated Parmesan cheese, if desired.

Chicken Alfredo

Ingredients:

- 2 tbsp olive oil
- 1 lb (450g) chicken breast, sliced into strips
- Salt and pepper to taste
- 2 cloves garlic, minced
- 1 cup heavy cream
- 1 cup grated Parmesan cheese
- 1/2 cup chicken broth
- 1 tsp dried Italian seasoning
- 1 lb fettuccine pasta
- 1 tbsp fresh parsley, chopped (optional)

Instructions:

1. **Cook the chicken**: Heat olive oil in a large pan over medium heat. Season the chicken with salt and pepper, then cook for 6-8 minutes until browned and cooked through. Remove the chicken and set it aside.
2. **Make the Alfredo sauce**: In the same pan, add garlic and sauté for 1 minute. Add the heavy cream, chicken broth, and Italian seasoning, stirring to combine. Bring to a simmer, then reduce heat and simmer for 5-7 minutes, allowing the sauce to thicken.
3. **Cook the pasta**: While the sauce is simmering, cook the fettuccine pasta according to package instructions. Drain and reserve 1 cup of pasta water.
4. **Combine and serve**: Add the cooked pasta to the sauce and toss to coat. Stir in the Parmesan cheese and reserved chicken, adjusting with pasta water as needed to reach the desired sauce consistency. Garnish with fresh parsley before serving.

Beef Tacos

Ingredients:

- 1 lb (450g) ground beef
- 1 packet taco seasoning (or homemade seasoning)
- 1/4 cup water
- 8 small taco shells or tortillas
- Toppings: shredded lettuce, diced tomatoes, shredded cheese, sour cream, salsa, jalapeños (optional)

Instructions:

1. **Cook the beef**: Heat a skillet over medium heat and brown the ground beef, breaking it up with a spoon as it cooks. Drain any excess fat.
2. **Add seasoning**: Stir in taco seasoning and water, cooking for another 5-7 minutes until the beef is fully cooked and the seasoning is well incorporated.
3. **Assemble the tacos**: Warm the taco shells according to package directions. Spoon the beef mixture into each shell, then top with your choice of lettuce, tomatoes, cheese, sour cream, salsa, and jalapeños.

BBQ Chicken Sliders

Ingredients:

- 2 cups cooked chicken, shredded (rotisserie chicken works great)
- 1 cup BBQ sauce
- 12 slider buns
- 1/2 cup shredded cheddar cheese
- 1/4 cup pickles (optional)

Instructions:

1. **Prepare the chicken**: In a bowl, toss the shredded chicken with BBQ sauce until well-coated.
2. **Assemble the sliders**: Place the bottom half of the slider buns on a baking sheet. Spoon the BBQ chicken mixture evenly over the buns, then top with shredded cheddar cheese. Place the top half of the buns on top.
3. **Bake**: Preheat the oven to 375°F (190°C). Bake the sliders for 10-12 minutes, until the buns are golden and the cheese is melted.
4. **Serve**: If desired, add pickles before serving for extra flavor.

Meatloaf with Mashed Potatoes

Ingredients:

- **For the meatloaf:**
    - 1 lb (450g) ground beef
    - 1 egg
    - 1/2 cup breadcrumbs
    - 1/4 cup milk
    - 1/4 cup onion, finely chopped
    - 2 cloves garlic, minced
    - 1 tsp salt
    - 1/2 tsp black pepper
    - 1/2 tsp dried oregano
    - 1/4 cup ketchup (for glaze)
- **For the mashed potatoes:**
    - 2 lbs (900g) potatoes, peeled and cubed
    - 1/2 cup milk
    - 4 tbsp butter
    - Salt and pepper to taste

Instructions:

1. **Prepare the meatloaf**: Preheat the oven to 375°F (190°C). In a bowl, combine the ground beef, egg, breadcrumbs, milk, onion, garlic, salt, pepper, and oregano. Mix well. Form the mixture into a loaf and place in a baking dish. Spread ketchup over the top for a glaze.
2. **Bake the meatloaf**: Bake in the preheated oven for 45-50 minutes, or until the meatloaf is cooked through and the internal temperature reaches 160°F (71°C).
3. **Make the mashed potatoes**: While the meatloaf bakes, bring a pot of salted water to a boil. Add the cubed potatoes and cook until tender, about 15 minutes. Drain and return to the pot. Mash with milk, butter, salt, and pepper until smooth.
4. **Serve**: Slice the meatloaf and serve with a generous scoop of mashed potatoes.

Chicken Parmesan

Ingredients:

- 4 boneless, skinless chicken breasts
- Salt and pepper to taste
- 1 cup flour
- 2 eggs, beaten
- 1 cup breadcrumbs (preferably Italian-style)
- 1 cup marinara sauce
- 1 1/2 cups mozzarella cheese, shredded
- 1/2 cup Parmesan cheese, grated
- Olive oil for frying

Instructions:

1. **Prepare the chicken**: Preheat the oven to 375°F (190°C). Season the chicken breasts with salt and pepper. Dredge each breast in flour, then dip in beaten eggs, and coat with breadcrumbs.
2. **Fry the chicken**: Heat olive oil in a large skillet over medium heat. Fry the chicken breasts for 3-4 minutes on each side until golden brown. Remove and set aside.
3. **Assemble and bake**: Place the fried chicken breasts in a baking dish. Spoon marinara sauce over each breast, then sprinkle with mozzarella and Parmesan. Bake for 20 minutes, or until the cheese is bubbly and the chicken reaches an internal temperature of 165°F (74°C).
4. **Serve**: Serve with pasta or a side salad.

Homemade Pizza

Ingredients:

- **For the dough**:
    - 2 1/4 tsp active dry yeast
    - 1 1/2 cups warm water
    - 1 tsp sugar
    - 3 1/2 cups all-purpose flour
    - 2 tbsp olive oil
    - 1 tsp salt
- **For the toppings**:
    - 1/2 cup pizza sauce
    - 1 1/2 cups shredded mozzarella cheese
    - Your choice of toppings (pepperoni, mushrooms, olives, peppers, etc.)

Instructions:

1. **Make the dough**: In a bowl, dissolve the yeast and sugar in warm water. Let it sit for 5-10 minutes until foamy. In a large bowl, combine the flour, olive oil, and salt. Add the yeast mixture and stir until a dough forms. Knead on a floured surface for 5-7 minutes, then place in an oiled bowl. Cover and let rise for 1 hour.
2. **Prepare the pizza**: Preheat the oven to 475°F (245°C). Punch down the dough and divide it into two portions. Roll out each portion into a circle. Place on a greased baking sheet.
3. **Assemble the pizza**: Spread pizza sauce over the dough, then top with mozzarella and your choice of toppings.
4. **Bake**: Bake for 10-15 minutes, until the crust is golden and the cheese is melted and bubbly.
5. **Serve**: Slice and serve hot.

Sloppy Joes

Ingredients:

- 1 lb (450g) ground beef
- 1 onion, finely chopped
- 1 bell pepper, chopped
- 1 can (8 oz) tomato sauce
- 1 tbsp Worcestershire sauce
- 2 tbsp ketchup
- 1 tbsp mustard
- Salt and pepper to taste
- 4 hamburger buns

Instructions:

1. **Cook the beef**: In a skillet, cook the ground beef over medium heat until browned. Drain excess fat.
2. **Add vegetables**: Add the chopped onion and bell pepper. Cook until softened, about 5 minutes.
3. **Add sauce**: Stir in tomato sauce, Worcestershire sauce, ketchup, mustard, salt, and pepper. Simmer for 10 minutes.
4. **Serve**: Spoon the mixture onto hamburger buns and serve.

Shepherd's Pie

Ingredients:

- 1 lb (450g) ground lamb (or beef)
- 1 onion, chopped
- 2 carrots, diced
- 1 cup frozen peas
- 2 tbsp tomato paste
- 1 cup beef broth
- 1/4 cup milk
- 4 cups mashed potatoes
- 1/2 cup shredded cheddar cheese (optional)

Instructions:

1. **Cook the filling**: In a large skillet, brown the ground lamb (or beef). Add onion, carrots, and peas, cooking until softened. Stir in tomato paste and beef broth, simmering until the mixture thickens, about 10 minutes.
2. **Assemble the pie**: Preheat the oven to 400°F (200°C). Transfer the meat mixture to a baking dish. Spread mashed potatoes evenly on top, smoothing with a spatula. Sprinkle with cheddar cheese if desired.
3. **Bake**: Bake for 20 minutes, until the top is golden.
4. **Serve**: Let cool slightly before serving.

Beef and Bean Chili

Ingredients:

- 1 lb (450g) ground beef
- 1 onion, chopped
- 2 cloves garlic, minced
- 1 can (15 oz) kidney beans, drained and rinsed
- 1 can (15 oz) black beans, drained and rinsed
- 1 can (14 oz) diced tomatoes
- 2 tbsp chili powder
- 1 tsp cumin
- 1 tsp paprika
- Salt and pepper to taste

Instructions:

1. **Cook the beef**: In a large pot, brown the ground beef over medium heat. Add the onion and garlic, cooking until softened.
2. **Add the beans and spices**: Stir in the kidney beans, black beans, diced tomatoes, chili powder, cumin, paprika, salt, and pepper. Bring to a boil, then reduce heat and simmer for 30-40 minutes, stirring occasionally.
3. **Serve**: Serve hot with toppings like sour cream, cheese, or chopped onions.

Chicken Stir-Fry

Ingredients:

- 1 lb (450g) chicken breast, thinly sliced
- 2 tbsp soy sauce
- 1 tbsp sesame oil
- 1 bell pepper, sliced
- 1 carrot, julienned
- 1/2 cup broccoli florets
- 2 cloves garlic, minced
- 2 tbsp oyster sauce
- 1 tbsp cornstarch (optional)

Instructions:

1. **Cook the chicken**: Heat sesame oil in a pan over medium-high heat. Add the chicken slices and cook until browned and cooked through, about 5-6 minutes.
2. **Add vegetables**: Add the bell pepper, carrot, broccoli, and garlic. Stir-fry for another 5 minutes until the vegetables are tender-crisp.
3. **Add sauce**: Stir in soy sauce, oyster sauce, and cornstarch (if using). Cook for 2-3 minutes until the sauce thickens.
4. **Serve**: Serve over rice or noodles.

Beef and Cheese Enchiladas

Ingredients:

- 1 lb (450g) ground beef
- 1 can (10 oz) enchilada sauce
- 1/2 cup onion, chopped
- 1 cup shredded cheddar cheese
- 8 corn tortillas
- Salt and pepper to taste

Instructions:

1. **Prepare the beef**: In a skillet, brown the ground beef over medium heat. Add onion and cook until softened. Stir in 1/4 cup of enchilada sauce, salt, and pepper.
2. **Assemble the enchiladas**: Preheat the oven to 375°F (190°C). Fill each tortilla with the beef mixture and cheese, rolling them up and placing them seam-side down in a baking dish.
3. **Top and bake**: Pour the remaining enchilada sauce over the tortillas and sprinkle with extra cheese. Bake for 20-25 minutes, until the cheese is melted and bubbly.
4. **Serve**: Serve hot with sour cream and salsa.

Grilled Cheese and Tomato Soup

Ingredients:

- **For the Grilled Cheese**:
    - 4 slices bread
    - 4 slices cheddar cheese
    - 2 tbsp butter
- **For the Tomato Soup**:
    - 1 can (28 oz) crushed tomatoes
    - 1 small onion, chopped
    - 2 cloves garlic, minced
    - 1 cup chicken broth
    - 1 tbsp olive oil
    - 1 tsp salt
    - 1/2 tsp black pepper
    - 1/2 cup heavy cream (optional)

Instructions:

1. **Make the soup**: Heat olive oil in a pot over medium heat. Add onion and garlic, cooking until softened, about 5 minutes. Add the crushed tomatoes, chicken broth, salt, and pepper. Bring to a simmer, then cook for 15 minutes. For a creamy version, stir in heavy cream just before serving.
2. **Prepare the grilled cheese**: Butter one side of each slice of bread. Place cheese between the slices, buttered side out. Grill on medium heat for 3-4 minutes per side, until golden brown and the cheese is melted.
3. **Serve**: Serve the grilled cheese with a bowl of hot tomato soup.

Fish Sticks with Fries

Ingredients:

- **For the Fish Sticks:**
    - 1 lb white fish fillets (such as cod or haddock), cut into strips
    - 1/2 cup flour
    - 2 eggs, beaten
    - 1 cup breadcrumbs
    - 1 tsp salt
    - 1/2 tsp black pepper
    - 1 tsp paprika
- **For the Fries:**
    - 4 large potatoes, peeled and cut into fries
    - 2 tbsp olive oil
    - Salt to taste

Instructions:

1. **Prepare the fries**: Preheat the oven to 425°F (220°C). Toss the potato fries in olive oil and salt. Arrange them in a single layer on a baking sheet. Bake for 25-30 minutes, flipping halfway, until crispy.
2. **Make the fish sticks**: Preheat oil in a skillet over medium heat. Dip fish strips in flour, then in beaten eggs, and coat with breadcrumbs mixed with salt, pepper, and paprika. Fry the fish sticks for 3-4 minutes per side, until golden and crispy.
3. **Serve**: Serve the fish sticks with the crispy fries and a side of tartar sauce.

Spaghetti Carbonara

Ingredients:

- 1 lb (450g) spaghetti
- 4 oz pancetta or bacon, diced
- 3 large eggs
- 1 cup grated Parmesan cheese
- 1/2 cup heavy cream (optional)
- 2 cloves garlic, minced
- Salt and black pepper to taste

Instructions:

1. **Cook the spaghetti**: Boil the spaghetti in salted water according to package instructions. Reserve 1 cup of pasta water before draining.
2. **Prepare the sauce**: In a skillet, cook the pancetta or bacon over medium heat until crispy, about 5 minutes. Add the garlic and cook for another minute. In a bowl, whisk together eggs, Parmesan, cream (if using), salt, and pepper.
3. **Combine**: Toss the drained pasta in the pancetta mixture, then quickly stir in the egg mixture, adding reserved pasta water a little at a time to create a creamy sauce.
4. **Serve**: Serve with extra Parmesan and black pepper.

Chicken Fajitas

Ingredients:

- 1 lb (450g) chicken breast, thinly sliced
- 1 onion, sliced
- 1 bell pepper, sliced
- 2 tbsp olive oil
- 1 tbsp chili powder
- 1 tsp cumin
- 1/2 tsp paprika
- Salt and pepper to taste
- 8 small flour tortillas
- Sour cream, salsa, and guacamole for serving

Instructions:

1. **Season the chicken**: In a bowl, toss the chicken with olive oil, chili powder, cumin, paprika, salt, and pepper. Let marinate for 10 minutes.
2. **Cook the chicken**: Heat a skillet over medium-high heat. Add the chicken and cook for 6-8 minutes, until browned and cooked through. Remove from the skillet and set aside.
3. **Cook the vegetables**: In the same skillet, add a bit more olive oil if needed, and cook the onion and bell pepper for 5 minutes, until softened.
4. **Serve**: Warm the tortillas and fill them with the chicken and vegetables. Serve with sour cream, salsa, and guacamole.

Macaroni and Cheese

Ingredients:

- 1 lb elbow macaroni
- 2 tbsp butter
- 2 tbsp flour
- 2 cups milk
- 2 cups shredded cheddar cheese
- Salt and pepper to taste

Instructions:

1. **Cook the macaroni**: Boil the elbow macaroni in salted water according to package instructions. Drain and set aside.
2. **Make the cheese sauce**: In a large pot, melt butter over medium heat. Stir in the flour to make a roux and cook for 1-2 minutes. Gradually whisk in the milk and cook until the sauce thickens, about 5 minutes. Stir in the cheddar cheese until melted and smooth.
3. **Combine**: Add the cooked macaroni to the cheese sauce and stir to combine. Season with salt and pepper.
4. **Serve**: Serve hot as a creamy side or main dish.

Teriyaki Chicken with Rice

Ingredients:

- 4 boneless, skinless chicken breasts
- 1/4 cup soy sauce
- 2 tbsp honey
- 2 tbsp rice vinegar
- 1 tbsp sesame oil
- 2 cloves garlic, minced
- 1 tsp fresh ginger, grated
- 2 cups cooked rice
- Sesame seeds and green onions for garnish

Instructions:

1. **Make the teriyaki sauce**: In a small saucepan, combine soy sauce, honey, rice vinegar, sesame oil, garlic, and ginger. Bring to a simmer and cook for 5-7 minutes, until the sauce thickens.
2. **Cook the chicken**: Grill or pan-sear the chicken breasts for 6-7 minutes per side, until cooked through.
3. **Serve**: Serve the chicken over a bed of cooked rice, drizzled with the teriyaki sauce. Garnish with sesame seeds and green onions.

Chicken Nuggets and Veggies

Ingredients:

- 1 lb (450g) chicken breast, cut into bite-sized pieces
- 1 cup breadcrumbs
- 1/2 cup flour
- 2 eggs, beaten
- Salt and pepper to taste
- 1 cup mixed vegetables (carrots, peas, etc.)
- Olive oil for frying

Instructions:

1. **Prepare the chicken nuggets**: Dredge chicken pieces in flour, dip in beaten eggs, and coat with breadcrumbs. Season with salt and pepper.
2. **Fry the nuggets**: Heat olive oil in a skillet over medium-high heat. Fry the chicken nuggets for 3-4 minutes per side, until golden and cooked through.
3. **Cook the veggies**: Steam or sauté the mixed vegetables until tender.
4. **Serve**: Serve the chicken nuggets with the veggies on the side, along with dipping sauces like ketchup or honey mustard.

Stuffed Bell Peppers

Ingredients:

- 4 bell peppers, tops cut off and seeds removed
- 1 lb (450g) ground beef or turkey
- 1 cup cooked rice
- 1/2 cup tomato sauce
- 1/2 cup shredded cheddar cheese
- 1 tsp garlic powder
- 1/2 tsp cumin
- Salt and pepper to taste

Instructions:

1. **Preheat the oven**: Preheat to 375°F (190°C).
2. **Prepare the filling**: In a skillet, cook the ground beef or turkey over medium heat until browned. Stir in the cooked rice, tomato sauce, garlic powder, cumin, salt, and pepper.
3. **Stuff the peppers**: Fill each bell pepper with the meat and rice mixture. Place the stuffed peppers in a baking dish and top with shredded cheese.
4. **Bake**: Cover with foil and bake for 25-30 minutes, then uncover and bake for an additional 5 minutes, until the cheese is melted and bubbly.
5. **Serve**: Serve hot with a side salad or bread.

Sausage and Peppers

Ingredients:

- 4 Italian sausages (mild or spicy)
- 2 bell peppers, sliced
- 1 onion, sliced
- 2 tbsp olive oil
- 2 cloves garlic, minced
- 1/2 tsp dried oregano
- Salt and pepper to taste
- 1/4 cup fresh parsley, chopped (optional)

Instructions:

1. **Cook the sausages**: In a large skillet, heat 1 tablespoon of olive oil over medium heat. Add the sausages and cook for about 10-12 minutes, turning occasionally, until browned and cooked through. Remove from the pan and set aside.
2. **Cook the vegetables**: In the same skillet, add another tablespoon of olive oil. Add the bell peppers, onion, and garlic. Sauté for 5-7 minutes, until the vegetables are tender.
3. **Combine and serve**: Slice the sausages and add them back to the pan with the peppers and onions. Stir in oregano, salt, and pepper. Cook for an additional 2-3 minutes. Garnish with parsley if desired. Serve hot.

Lasagna

Ingredients:

- 12 lasagna noodles, cooked and drained
- 1 lb ground beef or pork
- 1 onion, chopped
- 2 cloves garlic, minced
- 1 can (28 oz) crushed tomatoes
- 1 can (6 oz) tomato paste
- 1 tsp dried basil
- 1 tsp dried oregano
- 1/2 tsp salt
- 1/2 tsp black pepper
- 16 oz ricotta cheese
- 2 cups shredded mozzarella cheese
- 1/2 cup grated Parmesan cheese
- 1 egg

Instructions:

1. **Prepare the sauce**: In a large skillet, cook the ground beef with the onion and garlic until browned. Stir in crushed tomatoes, tomato paste, basil, oregano, salt, and pepper. Simmer for 20 minutes.
2. **Prepare the ricotta mixture**: In a bowl, combine the ricotta cheese, 1 cup of mozzarella, Parmesan, and egg. Mix well.
3. **Assemble the lasagna**: Preheat the oven to 375°F (190°C). In a baking dish, spread a thin layer of sauce on the bottom. Layer 3 lasagna noodles, followed by a third of the ricotta mixture, a third of the sauce, and a third of the remaining mozzarella. Repeat the layers twice, finishing with mozzarella on top.
4. **Bake**: Cover with foil and bake for 25 minutes. Remove the foil and bake for an additional 10-15 minutes, until bubbly and golden. Let rest for 10 minutes before serving.

Turkey Meatballs with Marinara

Ingredients:

- 1 lb ground turkey
- 1/4 cup breadcrumbs
- 1/4 cup grated Parmesan cheese
- 1 egg
- 2 cloves garlic, minced
- 1/4 cup parsley, chopped
- Salt and pepper to taste
- 2 cups marinara sauce
- Olive oil for frying

Instructions:

1. **Make the meatballs**: In a bowl, mix together ground turkey, breadcrumbs, Parmesan, egg, garlic, parsley, salt, and pepper. Shape the mixture into meatballs, about 1 inch in diameter.
2. **Cook the meatballs**: Heat olive oil in a skillet over medium heat. Add the meatballs and cook for 6-8 minutes, turning until browned on all sides.
3. **Simmer in marinara**: Pour the marinara sauce over the meatballs and simmer for 10-15 minutes, until the meatballs are cooked through.
4. **Serve**: Serve the meatballs with pasta, on a sub roll, or with a side of vegetables.

Pulled Pork Sandwiches

Ingredients:

- 3 lb pork shoulder
- 1 cup BBQ sauce
- 1/2 cup apple cider vinegar
- 1 onion, sliced
- 1 tsp smoked paprika
- 1 tsp garlic powder
- Salt and pepper to taste
- 4 hamburger buns
- Coleslaw for topping (optional)

Instructions:

1. **Cook the pork**: Season the pork shoulder with paprika, garlic powder, salt, and pepper. Place it in a slow cooker with the onion, BBQ sauce, and apple cider vinegar. Cook on low for 6-8 hours, until the pork is tender and easily shreds.
2. **Shred the pork**: Remove the pork from the slow cooker and shred it using two forks.
3. **Assemble the sandwiches**: Pile the shredded pork onto the hamburger buns and top with coleslaw if desired. Serve hot.

Veggie Fried Rice

Ingredients:

- 2 cups cooked rice (preferably cold)
- 1 cup mixed vegetables (carrots, peas, corn, etc.)
- 2 eggs, beaten
- 2 tbsp soy sauce
- 1 tbsp sesame oil
- 1/2 tsp garlic powder
- 1/2 tsp onion powder
- 2 tbsp vegetable oil

Instructions:

1. **Cook the vegetables**: Heat vegetable oil in a large skillet or wok over medium heat. Add the mixed vegetables and cook until heated through, about 5 minutes.
2. **Scramble the eggs**: Push the vegetables to the side of the skillet and pour the beaten eggs into the other side. Scramble the eggs until cooked through.
3. **Fry the rice**: Add the cold rice to the skillet, breaking up any clumps. Stir in the soy sauce, sesame oil, garlic powder, and onion powder. Cook for 5-7 minutes, until the rice is heated through and slightly crispy.
4. **Serve**: Serve the veggie fried rice hot as a side or main dish.

Beef Tacos with Guacamole

Ingredients:

- 1 lb ground beef
- 1 packet taco seasoning
- 1/2 cup water
- 8 taco shells
- 1 avocado, mashed
- 1 tbsp lime juice
- Salt to taste
- 1 cup shredded lettuce
- 1/2 cup diced tomatoes
- 1/2 cup shredded cheddar cheese

Instructions:

1. **Cook the beef**: In a skillet, cook the ground beef over medium heat until browned. Drain excess fat and stir in taco seasoning and water. Simmer for 5 minutes.
2. **Make the guacamole**: Mash the avocado and mix with lime juice and salt to taste.
3. **Assemble the tacos**: Spoon the beef mixture into the taco shells. Top with guacamole, shredded lettuce, diced tomatoes, and cheese.
4. **Serve**: Serve immediately with your favorite taco toppings.

Roast Chicken with Potatoes

Ingredients:

- 1 whole chicken (about 4 lbs)
- 2 tbsp olive oil
- 1 tsp rosemary
- 1 tsp thyme
- Salt and pepper to taste
- 4 large potatoes, cut into wedges
- 1 lemon, halved
- 4 cloves garlic, smashed

Instructions:

1. **Preheat the oven**: Preheat to 400°F (200°C).
2. **Prepare the chicken**: Rub the chicken with olive oil, rosemary, thyme, salt, and pepper. Place the lemon halves and garlic inside the chicken cavity.
3. **Roast the chicken**: Place the chicken on a roasting pan and surround it with potato wedges. Roast for 1 hour and 30 minutes, until the chicken is cooked through and the skin is crispy.
4. **Serve**: Let the chicken rest for 10 minutes before carving. Serve with the roasted potatoes.

Baked Ziti

Ingredients:

- 1 lb ziti pasta
- 1 lb ground beef or sausage
- 2 cups marinara sauce
- 16 oz ricotta cheese
- 2 cups shredded mozzarella cheese
- 1/2 cup grated Parmesan cheese
- 1 egg
- 1 tsp dried basil
- Salt and pepper to taste

Instructions:

1. **Cook the pasta**: Boil the ziti in salted water according to package instructions. Drain and set aside.
2. **Prepare the meat sauce**: In a skillet, cook the ground beef or sausage until browned. Stir in marinara sauce, basil, salt, and pepper. Simmer for 10 minutes.
3. **Make the ricotta mixture**: In a bowl, mix the ricotta cheese, egg, and half of the mozzarella.
4. **Assemble the ziti**: Preheat the oven to 375°F (190°C). In a baking dish, layer the pasta, ricotta mixture, meat sauce, and mozzarella. Repeat layers and top with Parmesan.
5. **Bake**: Cover with foil and bake for 25 minutes. Uncover and bake for an additional 10 minutes, until bubbly.
6. **Serve**: Serve hot with a side salad and garlic bread.

Shrimp Scampi

Ingredients:

- 1 lb shrimp, peeled and deveined
- 8 oz spaghetti or linguine
- 4 cloves garlic, minced
- 1/4 cup olive oil
- 1/4 cup unsalted butter
- 1/2 cup white wine (or chicken broth)
- 1/2 tsp red pepper flakes (optional)
- Salt and pepper to taste
- Juice of 1 lemon
- 1/4 cup fresh parsley, chopped

Instructions:

1. **Cook the pasta**: Boil water with salt, and cook the pasta according to package instructions. Drain and set aside.
2. **Cook the shrimp**: In a large skillet, heat olive oil and butter over medium heat. Add the garlic and red pepper flakes, and sauté for 1 minute until fragrant. Add the shrimp and cook for 2-3 minutes on each side, until pink and cooked through.
3. **Make the sauce**: Add white wine (or chicken broth) and lemon juice to the pan, and let it simmer for 2-3 minutes, scraping up any bits from the bottom.
4. **Combine**: Toss the cooked pasta into the skillet with the shrimp and sauce. Stir to coat the pasta in the sauce.
5. **Serve**: Garnish with fresh parsley and serve immediately.

Grilled Chicken Caesar Salad

Ingredients:

- 2 boneless, skinless chicken breasts
- 4 cups Romaine lettuce, chopped
- 1/2 cup Caesar dressing
- 1/4 cup grated Parmesan cheese
- Croutons (optional)
- 1 tbsp olive oil
- Salt and pepper to taste

Instructions:

1. **Grill the chicken**: Preheat the grill or grill pan over medium-high heat. Brush the chicken breasts with olive oil and season with salt and pepper. Grill for 6-8 minutes on each side, until the chicken is fully cooked. Let rest for 5 minutes before slicing.
2. **Assemble the salad**: In a large bowl, toss the chopped Romaine lettuce with Caesar dressing until evenly coated.
3. **Serve**: Top the salad with grilled chicken slices, Parmesan cheese, and croutons. Serve immediately.

Breakfast for Dinner (Pancakes, Eggs, Bacon)

Ingredients:

- **Pancakes**:
    - 1 1/2 cups all-purpose flour
    - 2 tbsp sugar
    - 1 tbsp baking powder
    - 1/2 tsp salt
    - 1 1/4 cups milk
    - 1 egg
    - 2 tbsp melted butter
- **Eggs**:
    - 4 eggs
    - 1 tbsp butter or oil
- **Bacon**:
    - 8 slices bacon

Instructions:

1. **Cook the bacon**: In a large skillet, cook the bacon over medium heat until crispy, about 4-5 minutes per side. Remove and drain on paper towels.
2. **Make the pancakes**: In a mixing bowl, whisk together flour, sugar, baking powder, and salt. Add the milk, egg, and melted butter, and stir until combined. Heat a griddle or skillet over medium heat and pour batter onto it. Cook for 2-3 minutes per side until golden brown. Keep warm.
3. **Cook the eggs**: In a separate skillet, heat butter or oil over medium heat. Crack the eggs into the skillet and cook to your preferred doneness (sunny side up, scrambled, etc.).
4. **Serve**: Serve the pancakes with eggs and bacon on the side.

Beef Burritos

Ingredients:

- 1 lb ground beef
- 1 packet taco seasoning
- 1/2 cup water
- 6 large flour tortillas
- 1 cup shredded cheese (cheddar, Mexican blend, etc.)
- 1/2 cup sour cream
- 1/2 cup salsa
- 1/4 cup chopped cilantro (optional)
- 1/4 cup sliced green onions (optional)

Instructions:

1. **Cook the beef**: In a skillet, cook the ground beef over medium heat until browned. Drain excess fat and stir in taco seasoning and water. Simmer for 5 minutes until well combined.
2. **Assemble the burritos**: Warm the flour tortillas in a skillet or microwave. Place a few spoonfuls of beef mixture in the center of each tortilla. Top with cheese, sour cream, salsa, and cilantro.
3. **Roll up the burritos**: Fold in the sides of the tortillas and roll them up tightly.
4. **Serve**: Serve the burritos hot with extra salsa or guacamole on the side.

BBQ Ribs with Corn on the Cob

Ingredients:

- 1 rack of baby back ribs
- 1 cup BBQ sauce
- 4 ears of corn, husked
- 2 tbsp butter
- Salt and pepper to taste

Instructions:

1. **Prepare the ribs**: Preheat the oven to 300°F (150°C). Season the ribs with salt and pepper and wrap them tightly in foil. Bake for 2.5-3 hours until tender.
2. **Grill the corn**: While the ribs are baking, preheat a grill to medium heat. Grill the corn for 8-10 minutes, turning every 2 minutes, until slightly charred. Brush with butter and season with salt and pepper.
3. **Glaze the ribs**: Remove the ribs from the oven and brush with BBQ sauce. Grill the ribs for 5-7 minutes, basting with more sauce, until caramelized.
4. **Serve**: Serve the ribs with grilled corn on the cob on the side.

Chicken and Rice Casserole

Ingredients:

- 2 cups cooked rice
- 1 lb chicken breasts, cooked and shredded
- 1 can cream of chicken soup
- 1/2 cup chicken broth
- 1 cup shredded cheddar cheese
- 1/4 cup grated Parmesan cheese
- Salt and pepper to taste
- 1/2 cup frozen peas (optional)

Instructions:

1. **Preheat the oven**: Preheat to 350°F (175°C).
2. **Mix the casserole**: In a large bowl, combine cooked rice, shredded chicken, cream of chicken soup, chicken broth, peas (if using), and 1/2 cup cheddar cheese. Season with salt and pepper.
3. **Bake**: Pour the mixture into a greased baking dish and top with remaining cheddar cheese and Parmesan. Bake for 20-25 minutes, until bubbly and golden.
4. **Serve**: Serve hot as a comforting, all-in-one meal.

Sliders with Sweet Potato Fries

Ingredients:

- **For the Sliders:**
    - 1 lb ground beef
    - 12 slider buns
    - 1/4 cup shredded cheese (optional)
    - Lettuce, tomato, pickles, and condiments
- **For the Sweet Potato Fries:**
    - 2 large sweet potatoes, peeled and cut into fries
    - 2 tbsp olive oil
    - 1 tsp paprika
    - Salt to taste

Instructions:

1. **Prepare the fries**: Preheat the oven to 425°F (220°C). Toss the sweet potato fries in olive oil, paprika, and salt. Spread them on a baking sheet and bake for 25-30 minutes, turning halfway through, until crispy.
2. **Make the sliders**: Form the ground beef into small patties and season with salt and pepper. Cook on a grill or skillet over medium-high heat for 3-4 minutes per side, until cooked through. Toast the slider buns on the grill or in a skillet.
3. **Assemble the sliders**: Place a beef patty on each bun and top with cheese, lettuce, tomato, and condiments of choice.
4. **Serve**: Serve the sliders with sweet potato fries on the side.

Beef Stroganoff

Ingredients:

- 1 lb beef sirloin or tenderloin, sliced thinly
- 2 tbsp butter
- 1 onion, chopped
- 2 cloves garlic, minced
- 1 cup beef broth
- 1 cup sour cream
- 1 tbsp Worcestershire sauce
- 1/2 tsp paprika
- 1 tbsp flour (optional)
- Salt and pepper to taste
- 8 oz egg noodles

Instructions:

1. **Cook the beef**: In a skillet, melt butter over medium heat. Add the sliced beef and cook for 3-4 minutes, until browned. Remove from the skillet and set aside.
2. **Cook the vegetables**: In the same skillet, add onions and garlic and sauté until softened, about 2-3 minutes.
3. **Make the sauce**: Add beef broth, Worcestershire sauce, paprika, and salt and pepper. Stir and bring to a simmer. If the sauce needs thickening, sprinkle in flour and whisk until smooth.
4. **Finish the dish**: Lower the heat and stir in the sour cream. Return the beef to the pan and cook for an additional 2-3 minutes.
5. **Serve**: Serve the stroganoff over cooked egg noodles.

Chicken Quesadillas

Ingredients:

- 2 chicken breasts, cooked and shredded
- 1 tbsp olive oil
- 1 small onion, diced
- 1 bell pepper, diced
- 1 cup shredded cheese (cheddar, Mexican blend, etc.)
- 4 flour tortillas
- 1/2 cup salsa
- Salt and pepper to taste
- Sour cream and guacamole for serving (optional)

Instructions:

1. **Cook the veggies**: Heat olive oil in a skillet over medium heat. Add the onion and bell pepper and sauté until softened, about 3-4 minutes. Season with salt and pepper.
2. **Assemble the quesadillas**: Place a tortilla in a separate skillet over medium heat. Sprinkle with a small amount of cheese, add a layer of shredded chicken, and top with sautéed vegetables. Add more cheese and top with another tortilla. Cook for 2-3 minutes per side until golden brown and the cheese is melted.
3. **Serve**: Slice the quesadillas into wedges and serve with salsa, sour cream, and guacamole.

Veggie Pizza

Ingredients:

- 1 pizza dough (store-bought or homemade)
- 1/2 cup pizza sauce
- 1 cup shredded mozzarella cheese
- 1/2 cup bell peppers, sliced
- 1/2 cup red onion, sliced
- 1/2 cup mushrooms, sliced
- 1/2 cup black olives, sliced
- 1/2 tsp dried oregano
- 1 tbsp olive oil

Instructions:

1. **Preheat the oven**: Preheat the oven to 475°F (245°C).
2. **Prepare the pizza**: Roll out the pizza dough on a floured surface to your desired thickness. Transfer the dough to a baking sheet or pizza stone. Spread pizza sauce evenly over the dough, leaving a small border.
3. **Top the pizza**: Sprinkle with mozzarella cheese, then add the sliced vegetables and olives. Sprinkle with oregano and drizzle with olive oil.
4. **Bake**: Bake for 12-15 minutes until the crust is golden and the cheese is bubbly.
5. **Serve**: Slice and serve immediately.

Turkey Burgers

Ingredients:

- 1 lb ground turkey
- 1/4 cup breadcrumbs
- 1/4 cup grated Parmesan cheese
- 1 tbsp Worcestershire sauce
- 1/2 tsp garlic powder
- 1/2 tsp onion powder
- Salt and pepper to taste
- 4 burger buns
- Lettuce, tomato, and condiments for serving

Instructions:

1. **Prepare the patties**: In a bowl, combine ground turkey, breadcrumbs, Parmesan cheese, Worcestershire sauce, garlic powder, onion powder, salt, and pepper. Mix until just combined. Form the mixture into 4 patties.
2. **Cook the burgers**: Heat a grill or skillet over medium heat. Cook the turkey burgers for 5-6 minutes per side, until fully cooked through (internal temperature of 165°F).
3. **Assemble the burgers**: Toast the burger buns. Place the turkey patties on the buns and top with lettuce, tomato, and condiments of choice.
4. **Serve**: Serve with your favorite sides like fries or a salad.

Chicken Tenders with Honey Mustard

Ingredients:

- 1 lb chicken tenders
- 1 cup breadcrumbs
- 1/2 cup flour
- 2 eggs, beaten
- Salt and pepper to taste
- 1/4 cup olive oil
- 1/2 cup honey
- 2 tbsp Dijon mustard
- 1 tbsp mayonnaise

Instructions:

1. **Bread the chicken**: Season chicken tenders with salt and pepper. Dredge in flour, dip in beaten eggs, and coat with breadcrumbs.
2. **Fry the tenders**: Heat olive oil in a skillet over medium heat. Fry the chicken tenders for 4-5 minutes per side until golden brown and cooked through. Drain on paper towels.
3. **Make the sauce**: In a small bowl, whisk together honey, Dijon mustard, and mayonnaise until smooth.
4. **Serve**: Serve the chicken tenders with the honey mustard dipping sauce on the side.

Beef and Vegetable Kabobs

Ingredients:

- 1 lb beef sirloin, cut into 1-inch cubes
- 1 bell pepper, cut into chunks
- 1 zucchini, sliced
- 1 onion, cut into chunks
- 1/4 cup olive oil
- 2 tbsp soy sauce
- 1 tbsp garlic powder
- 1 tsp dried oregano
- Salt and pepper to taste

Instructions:

1. **Marinate the beef**: In a bowl, combine olive oil, soy sauce, garlic powder, oregano, salt, and pepper. Add the beef cubes and mix to coat. Marinate for at least 30 minutes.
2. **Assemble the kabobs**: Thread the beef, bell pepper, zucchini, and onion onto skewers, alternating between meat and vegetables.
3. **Grill the kabobs**: Preheat the grill to medium-high heat. Grill the kabobs for 8-10 minutes, turning occasionally, until the beef reaches your desired level of doneness.
4. **Serve**: Serve the kabobs hot with a side of rice or salad.

Eggplant Parmesan

Ingredients:

- 2 medium eggplants, sliced into 1/2-inch rounds
- 2 cups marinara sauce
- 1 1/2 cups shredded mozzarella cheese
- 1/2 cup grated Parmesan cheese
- 2 eggs, beaten
- 1 cup breadcrumbs
- 1/4 cup flour
- Olive oil for frying
- Fresh basil for garnish (optional)

Instructions:

1. **Bread the eggplant**: Season eggplant slices with salt and let them sit for 20 minutes to draw out moisture. Rinse and pat dry. Dredge each slice in flour, dip in beaten eggs, and coat with breadcrumbs.
2. **Fry the eggplant**: Heat olive oil in a skillet over medium heat. Fry the eggplant slices for 2-3 minutes per side, until golden brown. Drain on paper towels.
3. **Assemble the dish**: Preheat the oven to 375°F (190°C). In a baking dish, spread a thin layer of marinara sauce. Layer fried eggplant slices, sauce, mozzarella, and Parmesan. Repeat until all ingredients are used.
4. **Bake**: Bake for 20-25 minutes, until the cheese is bubbly and golden. Garnish with fresh basil.
5. **Serve**: Serve with pasta or a side salad.

Chicken and Broccoli Alfredo Bake

Ingredients:

- 2 cups cooked chicken, cubed
- 3 cups broccoli florets, steamed
- 12 oz pasta (penne or rotini)
- 1 jar Alfredo sauce
- 1/2 cup grated Parmesan cheese
- 1 1/2 cups shredded mozzarella cheese
- Salt and pepper to taste

Instructions:

1. **Preheat the oven**: Preheat the oven to 350°F (175°C).
2. **Prepare the pasta**: Cook the pasta according to package directions. Drain and set aside.
3. **Assemble the bake**: In a large bowl, combine the cooked pasta, chicken, broccoli, and Alfredo sauce. Mix well and season with salt and pepper.
4. **Top the bake**: Transfer the mixture to a greased baking dish. Top with mozzarella and Parmesan cheese.
5. **Bake**: Bake for 20-25 minutes, until the cheese is melted and bubbly.
6. **Serve**: Serve hot, garnished with extra Parmesan if desired.

Meatball Subs

Ingredients:

- 1 lb ground beef
- 1/2 cup breadcrumbs
- 1/4 cup grated Parmesan cheese
- 1 egg
- 2 cloves garlic, minced
- 1 cup marinara sauce
- 4 sub rolls
- 1 1/2 cups shredded mozzarella cheese
- Fresh basil or parsley for garnish (optional)

Instructions:

1. **Make the meatballs**: Preheat the oven to 375°F (190°C). In a bowl, combine ground beef, breadcrumbs, Parmesan cheese, egg, and garlic. Season with salt and pepper. Form into 16 meatballs and place on a baking sheet.
2. **Cook the meatballs**: Bake for 20-25 minutes until cooked through.
3. **Assemble the subs**: Heat marinara sauce in a pot. Once meatballs are done, add them to the sauce and simmer for 5 minutes.
4. **Prepare the subs**: Slice the sub rolls and spoon meatballs and sauce into each roll. Top with mozzarella cheese.
5. **Melt the cheese**: Place the subs on a baking sheet and bake for 5 minutes until the cheese is melted.
6. **Serve**: Garnish with basil or parsley and serve immediately.

Beef and Spinach Lasagna Roll-Ups

Ingredients:

- 1 lb ground beef
- 1 jar marinara sauce
- 12 lasagna noodles, cooked
- 1 1/2 cups ricotta cheese
- 1 1/2 cups cooked spinach, drained and chopped
- 2 cups shredded mozzarella cheese
- 1/2 cup grated Parmesan cheese
- 1 egg
- Salt and pepper to taste

Instructions:

1. **Cook the beef**: Brown ground beef in a pan over medium heat. Add marinara sauce and simmer for 10 minutes.
2. **Prepare the filling**: In a bowl, combine ricotta cheese, spinach, egg, 1 cup mozzarella, and Parmesan. Season with salt and pepper.
3. **Assemble the roll-ups**: Lay out the cooked lasagna noodles and spread the cheese mixture evenly on each one. Roll up each noodle tightly.
4. **Bake**: Preheat the oven to 375°F (190°C). Spread a thin layer of marinara sauce on the bottom of a baking dish. Place the lasagna rolls in the dish, seam side down. Top with remaining marinara sauce and mozzarella.
5. **Cook**: Cover with foil and bake for 25 minutes, then uncover and bake for an additional 10 minutes.
6. **Serve**: Serve hot with extra Parmesan.

Chicken Pot Pie

Ingredients:

- 2 cups cooked chicken, diced
- 1 cup frozen peas and carrots
- 1/2 cup diced potatoes, cooked
- 1/4 cup butter
- 1/4 cup flour
- 1 1/2 cups chicken broth
- 1/2 cup milk
- 1 tsp dried thyme
- 1/2 tsp garlic powder
- Salt and pepper to taste
- 1 package refrigerated pie crusts (or homemade)

Instructions:

1. **Prepare the filling**: In a large saucepan, melt butter over medium heat. Stir in flour and cook for 1 minute. Gradually add chicken broth and milk, stirring constantly until thickened. Season with thyme, garlic powder, salt, and pepper.
2. **Add the chicken and veggies**: Stir in chicken, peas, carrots, and potatoes. Simmer for 5 minutes.
3. **Assemble the pie**: Preheat the oven to 400°F (200°C). Roll out one pie crust and place it in a 9-inch pie dish. Pour the chicken mixture into the pie crust. Top with the second crust, sealing the edges. Cut a few slits in the top to allow steam to escape.
4. **Bake**: Bake for 35-40 minutes until golden brown.
5. **Serve**: Let the pie cool for 5 minutes before slicing and serving.

Taco Salad

Ingredients:

- 1 lb ground beef
- 1 packet taco seasoning
- 4 cups lettuce, chopped
- 1 cup shredded cheese (cheddar or Mexican blend)
- 1/2 cup diced tomatoes
- 1/2 cup diced onions
- 1/4 cup black olives, sliced
- 1/2 cup sour cream
- 1/2 cup salsa
- Tortilla chips for topping

Instructions:

1. **Cook the beef**: Brown the ground beef in a skillet. Drain excess fat and add taco seasoning with 1/4 cup water. Simmer for 5 minutes.
2. **Assemble the salad**: In a large bowl, combine chopped lettuce, cheese, tomatoes, onions, and olives. Add the cooked beef on top.
3. **Serve**: Top with sour cream, salsa, and tortilla chips for crunch.

Pork Schnitzel with Mashed Potatoes

Ingredients:

- 4 boneless pork chops
- 1 cup flour
- 2 eggs, beaten
- 1 cup breadcrumbs
- 1/2 tsp paprika
- Salt and pepper to taste
- 2 tbsp butter
- 4 cups mashed potatoes (prepared)
- Fresh parsley for garnish (optional)

Instructions:

1. **Prepare the pork**: Season pork chops with salt, pepper, and paprika. Dredge in flour, dip in beaten eggs, and coat in breadcrumbs.
2. **Fry the schnitzel**: Heat butter in a large skillet over medium heat. Fry pork schnitzels for 4-5 minutes per side until golden brown and cooked through.
3. **Serve**: Serve the schnitzels on a plate with a generous portion of mashed potatoes. Garnish with fresh parsley.

Chicken Enchilada Casserole

Ingredients:

- 3 cups cooked chicken, shredded
- 1 can red enchilada sauce
- 1 cup shredded cheese (cheddar or Mexican blend)
- 8 corn tortillas, cut into strips
- 1/2 cup sour cream
- 1/4 cup chopped green onions

Instructions:

1. **Preheat the oven**: Preheat to 375°F (190°C).
2. **Assemble the casserole**: In a baking dish, layer corn tortilla strips, shredded chicken, enchilada sauce, and cheese. Repeat layers until all ingredients are used.
3. **Bake**: Cover with foil and bake for 20 minutes. Remove foil and bake for another 10 minutes until the cheese is bubbly.
4. **Serve**: Serve hot with a dollop of sour cream and chopped green onions.

Sweet and Sour Chicken with Rice

Ingredients:

- 1 lb chicken breast, cubed
- 1/4 cup cornstarch
- 2 tbsp olive oil
- 1 bell pepper, chopped
- 1 onion, chopped
- 1/2 cup pineapple chunks
- 1/2 cup sweet and sour sauce
- 2 cups cooked white rice

Instructions:

1. **Coat the chicken**: Toss chicken cubes in cornstarch until well coated.
2. **Cook the chicken**: Heat olive oil in a skillet over medium heat. Cook the chicken for 5-7 minutes until browned and cooked through.
3. **Add vegetables and sauce**: Add the bell pepper, onion, and pineapple chunks to the skillet. Pour in sweet and sour sauce and stir to combine. Simmer for 5 minutes.
4. **Serve**: Serve the sweet and sour chicken over cooked rice.

www.ingramcontent.com/pod-product-compliance
Lightning Source LLC
LaVergne TN
LVHW081325060526
838201LV00055B/2462